July - 1979

Bill –
        You need to show those cycles
whose boss or maybe stick with
the four wheel vehicle, the
kind that can't throw you!

Talks With God

        The whole class is thinking
and praying for your quick
recovery! God Bless!
        Your friends in Christ,
        The Kumjoynus Class!

Talks With God

The C.R. Gibson Company
Norwalk, Connecticut

Happy day feelings

I'm so happy today, God. And I'm not even sure why. This morning I woke up feeling very excited about life. I had that kind of tight, expectant feeling inside me, like all kinds of good things were coming my way.

Why am I so happy today?

No reason needed—sometimes just being alive is enough.

Thank you for giving me life. Today, especially, I really love it!

It's up to me

Dear God, I'm not asking for anything. Of course I always need your help, but right now what I really need to do is help myself.

More than ever, I'm convinced that I know what makes me happy and what makes me sad.

The choice is mine.

If I really want to be happy, I can be.

If I'm sad, that's my fault.

So no more complaints, no more self-pity. I want you near always but right now the help has to come from me.

The video trap

I've been watching too much TV again, God. And I feel bad about it.

Television is my security blanket. Whenever I'm feeling kind of down, I just plop myself in front of the tube and tune out the rest of the world. I'll watch old re-runs, silly game shows, anything. Sitting in front of that box, hour after hour, I'm like a vegetable. It makes me more depressed than ever.

Help me to get up and out and doing things, God. I want to be more than a viewer in this life.

I want to be a doer!

I'm human, too

Father, sometimes I think that being a minister must be one of the loneliest jobs in the world.

Oh, there are plenty of people in my life. But they all want my help—probably none of them could ever imagine that sometimes I need help myself.

The good people of my congregation love and respect me. But it's hard for any of them to really be my friend.

They don't understand that I need more than a spiritual life and conversations about the Bible. I need to live in this world, too . . . to talk about ordinary things, to get into arguments, to hear a joke even if it is on the salty side.

Perhaps people just naturally think of a minister as someone different, someone to be on guard with.

But ministers are just people like everyone else. We need laughter, understanding, sometimes help.

We know confusion, doubt, despair. And at those times we need people to talk to, frankly, openly, person to person.

Dear God, has much of the fault been mine? Do I seem kind of distant? Maybe my congregation thinks I want to be left alone. But I don't, God. I want to do your work and enjoy the blessings of friendship and companionship.

Help me to reach out more often. And help those I reach out to, to understand that I need help just as all men do, sometimes even more.

For a lost dog

You're busy, God, and this may seem like a small thing. But my parents said there was nothing too small to talk about with you.

My dog is lost. His name is Sam and he's not any special kind of dog. But he's special to me.

He ran away. I don't know why. But he's been gone for two days now.

Sam has lived with us for a long time. I know he likes it here. God, I miss him a lot and want him to come home again.

So this prayer is just for Sam. Help him find his way back home, God. Don't let him get run over by a car. Keep him safe. If he's hungry, will you help him find some food?

He's a good dog and hasn't ever done anything really bad. He has kind of fluffy gray hair and pointed ears.

Most of all, I want him back. But if he's wandered away too far and can't find his way, I hope that some other boy will find him and take care of him.

Wherever he is, please take care of him and tell him I love him a lot.

Thank you, God.

Amen

Prayer from suburbia

My life ought to be wonderful, God, but it's not. It's boring.

Out here in the suburbs it's safe and secure. We have this beautiful house and my husband is doing well, so we can afford a part-time maid.

That leaves me plenty of time for the hairdresser, the bridge club, tennis, luncheons, coffees and cocktails with my friends. Sometimes too many cocktails, I'm afraid.

Today I've been thinking—if I suddenly didn't exist any more, would it really make any difference?

Not really. It wouldn't make any difference because I don't do anything useful. Everything is coming in and nothing's going out.

I know you still love me, God, but how could you like me very much? I don't even like myself.

I'm like a piece of jewelry, expensive, decorative and basically useless.

If it sounds as though I'm complaining, I'm not. It's just that I'm angry with myself.

There are people here in this city I can help, God. Old people in homes who need someone to listen. Children who are sick or poor or without parents.

And that's my plan, God. I'm going to stop being bored and get to work.

It's not unselfish at all—I need to help people as much or more than they need me.

And I know that if I can do this, everything will be better. So help me, God, I don't want to be just another one of the "ladies who lunch". I want to be a useful, needed, feeling human being.

Green-eyed monster

Father, when my friend told me today about his new job and the big salary increase he was getting, I felt an emotion I was ashamed of.

I was jealous that he was doing so well, so much better than I am.

Oh, I acted pleased. I congratulated him. And, of course, a part of me was pleased; but deep down inside I was not truly 100% happy to hear the news.

I wouldn't feel so guilty if my envy had been directed toward anyone but my friend. If someone I knew only casually or someone I didn't like so well told me in a bragging way about an advancement, then at least my jealousy might have seemed more natural. Not OK, but more to be expected.

But this guy is my friend. He has always been on my side, helping me if I needed help. And he's always been sincerely glad when something good has happened to me.

So, why am I jealous? Am I just selfish? Is it my competitive spirit?

Being competitive is part of me and I'm not ashamed of it, but if I can't have friends who outdo me some-times, I'm going to wind up with a pretty mediocre bunch of friends.

Help me, Father, to do my best. But at the same time help me to be proud of the achievements of those I love. They're not out to get me. When they win, I win. I need that understanding in my heart so when I hear someone else's good news I will truly, totally rejoice along with them.

Dr. feel good

Today's world offers a lot of easy answers to nearly any problem. Almost every day I hear about some new short-cut to happiness.

We have TA and TM and EST. There are exercise plans, diets, creams, pills and all kinds of groups, programs and classes.

I've tried a few of the "new ways," God, and some of them aren't bad. But none of them seem to have a really long-lasting effect.

I'm beginning to think there isn't any easy answer— to see that the only way to happiness that works is your way. And it isn't so easy.

But I'm going to do my best, God. And I'm going to talk to you about it every day. With your help, I know that I can find what everyone seems to be looking for.

I won't have to fill in any coupons or pay any fees. All I'll have to do is live every day with your help, your guidance, your love.

They want a divorce

Today I got a letter from my son, God. He told me some news I've been afraid of hearing for months. He and his wife, whom I love like a daughter, are getting a divorce.

Why does this have to happen, God? They seem like such a perfect couple. And I love them both so much, want so much for them to be together.

My first impulse was to call or write a long letter and try to get them to wait, try to help them work things out.

But I know this isn't a step they have taken lightly. All the arguments I could present for staying together are probably ones they have thought of many times.

They've decided to part and even though it hurts me very deeply, this is a time when I must hold back, try not to interfere.

Be with them, Father. I know this is more painful for them than it is for me.

If there is any way they can reconcile their differences, help them to find that way. But if they have to part, I pray that they can do it without bitterness.

Help me, God, to try to change only those things which I can, to accept those things which I cannot change, and, through your wisdom, to always know the difference.

Every little bit hurts

Father, you know that I do very well when it comes to avoiding any major wrongdoing. I'm never tempted to kill another human being, to steal what isn't mine. I don't even cheat on my income tax.

It's the little things that trip me up. They seem so small and harmless that I do them without even thinking.

When I hear an interesting story about someone, I almost always repeat it. It rarely occurs to me to check it out or to just plain keep my mouth shut. Result: Gossip.

My family is sometimes careless around the house. Now I know that's not a big deal. But there are days when I find wet towels on the bathroom floor, coats tossed over chairs and dirty glasses under the bed and I can't control my anger. Result: Complaints, nagging.

When someone calls to ask me to join a club or do some volunteer work, I never feel that I can simply refuse. It seems so rude. So I make up some excuse. Result: Lie.

Father, these are only little sins but put together they add up to a side of my personality I don't like very much.

I'm going to try and be more careful, God. Please forgive me when I slip up. Please help me to remember that what seems like a small wrong to me may end up making me look like a pretty small person.

A day brightener in my mail box

Dear God, the mail just came and turned my day around. I wasn't in a very good mood. There were so many things facing me that I didn't want to do. But the mailman left me a happy surprise. There, in the middle of the bills and the circulars, was a pale blue envelope. The familiar handwriting told me it was a letter from my friend, Mary.

Getting that letter was like a sudden burst of sunshine on this gloomy day. And I really didn't even deserve it. I've been owing her a letter for weeks and now I owe her two. But that's the kind of friend she is. She never keeps score. She just keeps on writing, no matter how far behind I get.

Mary knows me so well, tells me so many things I want to hear. And she always has a funny story to share.

I'm going to read that long, newsy letter one more time and then I'm going to sit down and write her an even longer one.

Thank you, God, for giving me a friend like Mary. One who, no matter how far apart we are or how long we go without seeing each other, always seems near to me.

On my daughter's wedding day

In just a few minutes I'm going to be a mother-in-law, God.

People always say—"A son is a son till he takes a wife, but a daughter's a daughter all of her life."

There's some truth in that, I suppose. But things are going to be different now. Her husband will come first in my daughter's life, and that's the way it should be.

Father, I don't want to be the kind of woman that mother-in-law jokes are made of. Those jokes really aren't funny.

My daughter and her new husband are just starting out today. They're so young. They're bound to make some mistakes. But help me to mind my own business, Lord. Hold me back from rushing in too often and trying to help too much.

If they have arguments and misunderstandings, which of course they will, I don't want to ever take sides. Nor do I ever want to give the impression that my daughter has a standing invitation to "come home to mother" at the least sign of trouble.

I want to help them all I can, if they really need and want my help.

And if grandchildren come along—oh, I hope they do!—let me love them without ever trying to take over the business of raising them.

I've had a mother-in-law now for almost 30 years.

The best way for me to say how I want to be is that I want to be like her.

She's always been so tactful and understanding. Even during the year when my husband was out of work, and we went to live with her, she always loved us but she left us alone as much as possible.

She must have had your help, Father, to be such a wonderful mother-in-law. I want to be like her, good and wise, loving and loveable, the kind of a mother-in-law who really is almost like a Mother.

The new job jitters

I'm really nervous this morning, God—so uptight that I've been awake since 5 o'clock. My stomach is tied up in knots. And my mind seems glued to the day ahead—my first day on the new job.

It's silly to be upset, but I can't help it. I feel like I did years ago when my parents moved and I had to go to a new school.

What if I don't wear the right kind of clothes and do all the wrong things? What if the people don't like me? What if I can't learn how to do the work?

Maybe the people I'm going to meet will remember how they felt when they were just starting out. Then if I make a fool of myself, it won't matter so much.

If I can just relax and be myself, maybe things will be all right.

Might as well get up now. Just lying here worrying is no help. And maybe a long, hot bath will help me out of the jitters.

I'm going to be calling on you all day, God. Please be there beside me. Then I won't feel so alone in a strange place. And maybe tonight I'll know that there wasn't any reason to be afraid, that everything really is going to be all right.

Up and down feelings

I have these mood swings, God. They're really strange.

Sometimes I feel like I've really got it all together and then the next minute, for some insignificant reason, or for no reason at all, I start feeling like I'm ugly and useless and unloveable.

My parents say I'm just going through a phase. And they're really patient with me and understanding.

But I don't like myself very much when I get to feeling so low.

I'm going to work at it, God—getting through this "phase" I'm going through.

And when the bad moods get me down, I'll be counting on you to help me get back up again.

Thanks, God, for listening.

In the election booth

Just a brief word of thanks, God, for the opportunity to come into this booth and tell my country what I think about things.

This moment always kind of gets to me. And I think it always will, no matter how many elections I vote in.

I'm very proud, very grateful to live in the United States of America. You truly have blessed our country and I pray that you always will.

Help me now to vote for the best possible leaders. It's an old cliché, but I really do want the best men and women to win because, if they do, then America will win, too.

Boomerang

I hurt my Mother, God, and now I'm hurting, too.

I felt like she had been on my back all day, telling me to pick up my clothes and empty the dishwasher while I was talking on the phone.

My anger just kept building up until I yelled at her and told her to quit bugging me.

I thought she would come right back at me, but she didn't. She just turned away, as if I had slapped her and she didn't want me to see her tears.

Now that moment is going through my head over and over again, like a bad movie.

I should have told her I was sorry right away, but I didn't. Maybe I wanted to punish myself by keeping the hurt inside. But I'm hurting her, too, by waiting.

Now I'm going to make things right. I'm going to go in the kitchen and give her a big hug and tell her how much I love her. Go with me, God. I want your love to go along with mine so she'll know that I'm really sorry, that I didn't mean it, that I really care.

A prayer from the heart

This prayer is going to be different, God.

I realized today what I've been doing. Every time I pray, I always begin with a prayer left over from my childhood. All I do is repeat some words I've said so often that they've lost most of their original meaning and beauty.

I don't even think about what I'm saying anymore. Those words come only from memory, never from my heart.

Then I get to the part where I say the things I think I'm supposed to say.

I praise you and thank you for all you've given me. Then I ask you to be good to my parents, my friends. Even people in other countries who are having a hard time. This is pretty phony praying, God.

The part where I really pay attention to what I'm saying comes at the end when I start asking for things. You know how it always goes.

I want something pretty badly, so I ask you for it. Then I promise that if you give it to me, I'll give you something in return. Like maybe I'll promise to be nice to mother and help her around the house for a whole year.

Tacked onto that promise is a threat. I never say it, but you know it's there. It's sort of the very fine print in the contract—that if you don't give me what I want, I won't love you any more.

You still love me, don't you God? I don't see how you can, but I believe you do.

Well, from now on I'm going to be more deserving of your love.

No more memorized prayers, no more phony prayers and no more deals.

Oh, I'll still be asking you for things. But when I do there won't be any strings attached.

From now on I'm going to try and talk with you naturally and honestly, without doing any bargaining, straight from my heart.

I promise.

Loving too late

I'm feeling very sad today, God. And very ashamed of myself.

I just came back from my grandmother's funeral.

While I was sitting there listening to the music, I started thinking of how much she loved me and of how seldom I spent any time with her in the last few years.

When I was little I used to stay with her a lot. But the older I got, the more I tried to avoid her.

It seemed she wanted too much from me. I often felt trapped with her, as though I couldn't breathe.

She was so slow and told long stories that I'd heard many times before. Her house smelled funny. It had an "old person smell." And I didn't like it when she wanted to sit next to me and put her arm around me.

If I could go back in time, I would make it up to her, God. Because I did love her a lot. I still do.

Please tell her that for me, God. Tell her I miss her very much and that I'll try to be extra nice to my family if that can help me make it up to her.

Prayer for sleep

It's 3 a.m., God, and I haven't slept a wink.

These are the loneliest times of all for me. I feel as if everyone else in the world is asleep and at peace, while I'm all by myself, struggling in the darkness.

My mind keeps churning and I can't make it stop. It rushes from one thought to another. Things I've avoided thinking about for days come to me clearly now. Some of my thoughts are dark and frightening. It's almost like having nightmares while I'm still awake.

No matter how I turn, I can't seem to find a comfortable position.

Counting sheep won't help. Sleeping pills can knock me out, but they never give me the good, restful, dreaming sleep I need.

Please help me to sleep, God. Relax my body. Slow my mind. Give me your peace.

Just talking to you is helping. I feel calmer now. I'm going to say your prayer now, God. It always helps me somehow.

The Lord is my Shepherd; I shall not want.

He maketh me to lie down in green pastures.

He leadeth me beside the still waters.

He restoreth my soul . . .

What color are you, God?

I'm black, God. What color are you?

A lot of people think you are a very old man with a long, white beard. That's OK if that's the way you look, but I don't think you do.

Are you a man or a woman?

Are you black?

Or yellow or brown?

I know you won't tell me because you don't tell people things any more like you did in the Bible. Why is that, God?

I would really like to see you, God. If you were black that would make me feel glad because you would be more like me.

If you want to know, I'll tell you what I think you look like. I don't think you're black or white or any color at all. And you're not a man or a woman.

I think you look like someone nobody has ever seen before. Not scary, though.

If love was something we could see, I think love is what you would look like.

I just wanted to tell you that.

I love you.

Amen

Rich man – Poor man

It's been a long time since I've talked to you, God.

I've been so busy for so many years, working hard to reach the goals in life I had set.

It was the American dream I was after, God. And now that dream is finally a reality . . . the beautiful home full of expensive furniture, television sets, stereo, every kind of modern appliance . . . enough money now to have a pool in the back yard, a cabin on the lake, a boat. The cars are the flashiest, the clothes are the finest. It's really "the good life"—on the outside anyway.

But it's not good enough, God. A lot of years have been traded for those material things and now they don't seem to mean much.

My family has had everything they could want—except me and my love. In the process of making money I've made myself a stranger to my wife and children.

There's got to be more to life, God. I'm going to start looking for it. Help me find myself again. Help me slow down.

Give me the patience to take time to stop and smell the flowers, to really talk to my kids, to show my wife I do love her.

Help me, Lord, to feel again. I don't want to wind up an old man who looks back and thinks—"Is that all there is?"

Please give me the time. Please give me your help.

There will be a next time

I've failed at what I set out to do, God. My business looked like a sure thing in the beginning. But so many things went wrong. Now the company is being sold to pay the bills. And so much of the money and time I've invested is lost.

Thinking about what went wrong, one thing stands out. When I started this venture, my main interest was making a lot of money. That was the aim, above and beyond just working hard to do my very best, to do something to be proud of. I think if I had approached it that way, everything might have been different. At least I gained that knowledge and next time things will be different as a result of it.

There will be a next time, God. I'm already excited about starting again!

One of my biggest fears when I saw that this was tumbling down around me, was—what will everyone think? I'd talked so much, even bragged, about all the *great things I was going to accomplish. And I've been afraid that my family and friends might be ashamed of me, that some of them might laugh, even be a little pleased that I got my comeuppance.*

But I was wrong. There hasn't been any humble pie to eat. No laughter. Only genuine regret that things didn't work out for me.

The people who care for me are a lot more loving and supportive than I gave them credit for. That's another thing I learned out of all this disappointment.

It's not easy to fail, God. But now I feel closer to you. Partly because I realize now how much I need your help.

You've given it to me already. Thank you, God. Thank you for showing me that there's a big difference between failing and being a failure.

Now I'm ready to try again. I think that this time, together, we're going to succeed.

Happy 40th?

It's here and there's no avoiding it . . . how I've been
dreading this day!

It's my 40th Birthday, God. A lot of friends and
loved ones have remembered me with cards and phone
calls and gifts. This gives me a bittersweet pleasure.

It's always nice to be remembered, but I was hoping that this particular birthday could come and go without much fanfare.

This birthday, the 40th, must be the one that women look forward to the least. For men, I guess it's the 50th and that doesn't seem very fair, but that's the way it is.

A lot of women think that being 40 means saying goodbye to youth, beauty and romance. I share some of those feelings, God. If I could be 29 again that might be nice. At least it would be more fun to look in the mirror every morning.

But as I think about it, along with the Goodbye's (and I'm not saying any until I have to) there are Hello's to be said today.

I feel an assurance in myself, as a woman, as a person, that I've never felt so strongly before.

I'm fairly satisfied with the past 40 years and am looking forward to 40 more, if that's your plan.

In the future, I have love, friendship, laughter, work and accomplishment to look forward to.

As I've gained the crow's-feet and those few extra pounds, I've lost many of my uncertainties about life, about myself . . . about my faith in you, God.

I'm strong, healthy and very richly blessed. Thank you, Father.

So I'm ready for this day. They can bring in the cake and put all 40 candles on it if they can find room.

Happy 40th? Yes!

A father's prayer

I'm worried about my son, God.

Now that he's a teenager we seem to be having a hard time communicating. I just can't get through to him.

It's really for his own good when I try to discipline him. But he can't see it that way. He thinks I'm against him, that I don't love him. A lot of times, he doesn't even think I know what I'm talking about.

I remember having some of those same feelings about my own father. He didn't seem too bright to me back when I was 17 and on top of everything. Of course, I was wrong. About both of us. But that knowledge didn't really come to me until I was grown and had children of my own.

The world has changed so much and there are so many dangers and temptations facing kids today. I don't want to wait for my son to become an adult before he starts liking me again.

I want his love and respect now so I can help him over some of the rough spots.

Have I been listening enough, God? He doesn't seem to think so.

I'm going to try every way I know to grow close to him again, God. I'll spend more time with him and really listen to what he's trying to tell me.

Help me to be more understanding, God, to not lose my temper.

I know this isn't going to be an easy job. Maybe I won't succeed. But I'm going to keep trying.

Help me be a good father to my son, God. Help me to help him.

I can't help wondering

I'm almost afraid to ask you any questions, God. In church they talk about just believing and not questioning anything. My parents say the same thing.

Well, I do believe in you. But there are so many things I can't figure out.

If you love everyone, why do you let some people go to hell and burn for eternity? You can do anything, so why don't you give them another chance?

Another thing, it seems like some of us get a better chance to go to Heaven. I have a better chance than a little boy born in India, who was an orphan maybe and so hungry he had to steal his food. If he went to hell for that, it wouldn't seem fair.

How long is eternity? Can things really go on forever? Does the universe go on forever? That idea really bothers me. Thinking about anything so big as the universe is kind of scary. And if it doesn't go on forever, if it stops, then what is there? I can't imagine just nothing.

Did someone or some power make you, God? Or have you just always been?

Those are the questions that bother me, God. If you don't want me to know the answers, I'll probably keep on thinking about them. But I won't get mad about not knowing.

I just wanted to say those things even though I know you know they're on my mind.

If I've talked about things I'm not supposed to, please forgive me. I just don't understand and wanted to talk.

Goodnight, God.

So many miracles

Just now, when I went out to get the morning paper, God, everything smelled fresh, rain-washed clean. Usually I just run out and back. But today I'm glad I stopped, looked, smelled, listened.

Everywhere I found beauty . . . jonquils blooming, birds singing, the sun shining gloriously. All that new life around me told me that the long winter is finally over. It's spring again.

It really struck me that I was witnessing hundreds of miracles. Right now. Today. In my own front yard!

Every blade of grass, each budding branch, all the dew drops sparkling with sunshine are miracles. I've just been too busy to see what is going on all around me.

Thank you, God, for slowing me down for a moment to take a good look at this beautiful world. Thank you for so many miracles that strengthen my faith and make me secure in your love.

I hate you, Mommy

She's only five years old, God. But today when she said, "I hate you, Mommy!" it really hurt.

Probably every child says those words at one time or another along the way of growing up. But when they're directed at you it's a painful experience.

Of course she doesn't really hate me, although just for that moment she surely did. And I don't blame her for that flash of anger—I can't blame her because I recognize the feeling and it's time to acknowledge it— I've experienced the same kind of anger toward her many times.

Why is it so difficult for me to admit the negative emotions my child can cause? Perhaps it's because I really want the best for her and the best certainly doesn't include a mother who loses her temper like a child!

I love her more than anyone else in the world, God, but there are times when she makes me explode inside. Instead of wanting to hug her, I want to shake her.

Getting along with a child is so different than it is with another adult. She doesn't look at life the way I do. But what I need to remember is that this makes things difficult for both of us.

So many things can go wrong during the course of a day. If I'm busy working and she demands more attention than I can spare, anger starts to build up in me. That's when I need to stop and talk things out with you, God.

That's when I need to let her know that the negative feelings in me that she must sense, don't mean that I love her any the less.

Right now, I want to make it easy for her to set things right with me. The hurt has gone out of me and I'm only concerned with what she must be feeling.

Help her to know that the Mommy she sometimes hates understands where those feelings come from.

I love her so much. And she loves me, too. Help us both to be patient, growing closer to each other as we grow closer to you and your love.

For the rest of my life

Getting old is one of those things I thought would never happen to me. But it has happened, God. Now a flight of stairs leaves me winded; I've started repeating myself, forgetting things that happened only yesterday. And when I look at that face in the mirror every morning—there's no getting around it. I'm getting old.

I've known lots of old people. A few of them were full of life right up to the last. But some didn't do very much with the rest of their lives.

I've been thinking about being old, God. Since that's what I am, I want to be good at it. In fact, I've thought of some things I can do to keep me young on the inside where it counts.

There will be times when I'm not feeling so hot, God. Help me to keep it to myself. Nothing is more boring than a long description of illnesses, real or imagined.

As long as I can be up and out, that's where I want to be. I want to stay active and useful as long as I can. There are people out there I can help, maybe just by being there, talking, listening, caring. The pay's no good, but I think I'll like the work.

God, help me to love my family, but never to demand their love in return. If I'm the right kind of person, that love will come naturally. I won't have to ask for it. It will be there.

There are a lot of things about being old that are really pretty funny, God. I don't want to forget that. I want to have a good laugh every chance I get. And if the joke's on me, well that's fine, too.

That's about it for now, God. I'm feeling closer to you all the time. But until we finally do get together, I want to do my best to be what the kids call—"an oldie, but a goodie!"

I like you, God

Before I go to sleep, I want to tell you that I really do like you, God. And I'm not just saying that because I want you to give me something.

Thank you for all the stuff you've given me already.

I like this world you made. There's a lot of things about it I don't understand yet—like, how come if it's spinning around so fast all the people don't fly off? You must keep us on. Thank you for that, too.

I like summertime because I can go swimming a lot. When you made all the water, did you think about how much fun kids would have in it? Pools are OK but the ocean is really great!

I like all the trees because I can climb up in them and even build a treehouse.

Now I have two friends. Did you tell them to like me? Having friends makes me feel happy.

My Mother and Dad are good to me and if I get scared in the night they get me unscared.

There's a lot more but I'm getting sleepy. I guess you know anyway.

God, I like you a whole lot!

He doesn't love me

He doesn't love me, God. He doesn't even like me.

I wanted him to love me so much, God. And I've asked you to make him love me, even though that didn't seem really fair. I guess you thought so, too.

I was just so full of feeling that I couldn't help talking about it. When his friends found out, they started kidding him about it. Then today, he told me that I was acting pretty silly, that I should stop talking about him and quit hanging around all the time.

I'm so embarrassed. Everyone knows. If only I hadn't been so open about the way I felt. But I couldn't keep all that love a secret.

God, I remember something my father used to tell me when I was a little girl. If I fell and skinned my knee, he would tell me that "it will feel so much better when it stops hurting."

I hope that's the way it's going to be for me now. Make it stop hurting soon, God. And when it does, maybe I'll have grown up a little. Maybe I'll feel even better than before, patient but ready to love again when love is ready for me.

An anniversary prayer

Today is our 5th wedding anniversary, God. And I've been thinking how different we are from the bride and groom of years ago.

Our marriage is a good one. We're happy. But five years have changed us both in many ways. It has happened so slowly that we're scarcely aware of it.

Some of the dreams we once shared have been discarded, forgotten. The excitement, the newness of our love has worn off because of the everydayness of our lives.

Father, I want to begin again on this anniversary. I want to get to know my husband all over again.

We know each other so well now that we hardly ever talk the way we used to. So many things go unspoken because each of us knows how the other feels.

I want to talk to him again. Really communicate. And I think he'd like that, too.

I want us to talk more about the feelings we have and not so much about bills and ills.

He's such a wonderful man. I love him more than ever. And I want to tell him that. It's nice to hear things spoken even if you already know them in your heart.

Being his wife has made me very proud and happy. I want to make sure he knows that.

Thank you for these 5 years, Father. May we have many more together. And help us grow kinder to each other, more responsive, more supportive and understanding, more feeling, more loving through every year we share.

Why aren't you married?

Today I heard the same old question, God—"Why doesn't a pretty woman like you settle down, get married and raise a bunch of kids?"

My answer—"Because I don't want to."—must sound rude. But it's the truth.

Father, you know that I decided a long time ago that if love and marriage came that would be fine. But life as a single woman seems to suit me just fine right now.

Help my well-meaning friends and relatives, God. I want them to understand that I'm contented and fulfilled with my life.

I don't want them to worry about me. And, at the same time, I don't want to be prodded all the time to do "what every woman was created for."

To the best of my understanding, you created me to be me. That's what I'm doing and I like it.

Thank you, God, for giving me the insight and the courage to choose my own way of life. Doing it my way has made me a very happy woman.

The word that hurts

My dad said "Nigger" today. He was telling a joke that started out, "Did you hear the one about the nigger and the . . ."

Pretty soon everyone was laughing. Everyone but me.

I've tried to talk to him about that word and some of the others he uses without thinking—"Wop," "Kike," "Polock." But it just makes him mad. He thinks I'm preaching to him. That I have a "holier than thou" attitude.

That's not the way it is at all, God. I don't think I'm better or smarter than my Dad.

But he grew up when the world was different. And I think there are some things about people's feelings that he doesn't understand.

Help me, God, to help him without making him resentful. Help me to make him hear just how hard and cruel that word "Nigger" sounds.

The here and now

There's a dumb thing I do, God. My parents have told me about it but I didn't listen for a long time. Now I know they're right.

The problem is that I'm only interested in "what's next." The worst thing about it is that it really takes the fun out of whatever I'm doing.

If I go to the movies, I start thinking about how I'd like to be swimming. Then if I go swimming, I start wishing I could go roller skating. No matter what I'm doing, I'm not satisfied. Isn't that crazy?

Well, I'm going to work on that one. I'm going to try and concentrate on what's happening right now.

Right now I'm talking to you. All of me. It's better that way.

Talking with God

I don't know how to pray the fancy way, God. The way the minister prays in church with all the "Thee's" and "Thou's."

Prayers like that sound almost too perfect. Even a little bit phony because you know they have to be carefully planned and rehearsed in advance.

I don't know how to pray that way and I really don't want to learn. I just want to talk to you, simply, in my own words. That's the only way I can say all the things I want to tell you.

Is that OK, God? Can I talk to you the way I would talk to a very good friend?

Something tells me that you may like that kind of prayer best of all.

And God created laughter

Thank you for laughter, God. It's one of the best things you ever dreamed up.

I think the greatest high in the world is just when I get together with my friends and we talk and tell jokes and laugh until we're falling out of our chairs.

I don't even mind when I do something crazy and everyone laughs at me. I can laugh at myself.

Do you ever get kind of tickled at some of the strange things you see going on down here? I think you must. Because laughter must have come from you in the first place.

And when something really funny happens, that doesn't hurt anyone, I'll bet you're laughing right along with the rest of us.

Some people might think that idea is sacrilegious, but not me. I think that laughter is an important part of love and since you are love, well . . .

Written by Dean Walley

Design: Al Petersen
Illustration: Blanche L. Sims